Original title:
Photosynthesis of the Soul

Copyright © 2025 Creative Arts Management OÜ
All rights reserved.

Author: Sophia Kingsley
ISBN HARDBACK: 978-1-80566-592-2
ISBN PAPERBACK: 978-1-80566-877-0

Fragrance of Freedom

In gardens where we dream and play,
The flowers dance, come what may.
A bumblebee's got moves so slick,
He's shaking it—oh, what a trick!

We sip the nectar, feeling bold,
Two robins twirl—if truth be told.
They gossip 'bout the sun's great shine,
And squawk about that grapevine wine!

Sunlit Reflections

A squirrel prances on the lawn,
Stealing rays from dusk till dawn.
With shades on, he struts like a star,
Yelling, "Look at me, I'm bizarre!"

The daisies giggle in the breeze,
"I'll go viral—just wait, please!"
Mirror, mirror, on the grass,
Who's the silliest? "Oh, that lass!"

Embers of Enlightenment

The ants hold meetings late at night,
Debating who's the fastest flight.
With tiny briefcases, they convene,
Comparing lunch—an ant's cuisine!

A ladybug takes the mic with glee,
"Let's all start a dance-off, just you and me!"
Sparkles fly from every wing,
Life's a hoot when we can sing!

The Vital Breath

Inhaled giggles, exhaled sighs,
Breath of laughter fills the skies.
A wind-up toy just lost control,
And wobbles 'round—oh, what a role!

The sun yawns big, a golden tease,
While clouds engage in pillow ease.
"Let's bounce around and have some fun!"
Nature's circus has just begun!

Dance of Light and Spirit

Sunbeams jiggle on the leaves,
Catch a breeze, do the weave.
Grass blades twirl in joyful glee,
Nature's dance, wild and free.

Laughter in the petals' hum,
Buzzy bees go thrum-thrum-thrum.
Jumping jacks from trees above,
All are sharing light and love.

Whispering Green Heartbeats

The trees gossip, "Did you see?"
Roots are tickling, full of glee.
With every rustle, laughter spreads,
Nature's pulse beneath our heads.

Frogs croak jokes by the pond's edge,
While flowers smile and take the pledge.
To spread joy in the summer air,
With green heartbeats everywhere.

Sunlit Paths of Inner Growth

On sunlit trails, the shadows prance,
While dandelions join the dance.
Each step is light, each giggle bright,
As sunflowers stretch to greet the light.

Wiggly worms in hats so fine,
Claim the ground as their own line.
With every step, we learn to sway,
In this playful, sunny ballet.

The Alchemy of Light and Life

Turnip tops wear crowns, so grand,
Sunshine sips from nature's hand.
Mixing rays and giggles too,
Creating shades of every hue.

Bubbles rise from muddy pools,
Where laughter hides and sunlight rules.
Who knew life could be such fun?
In this garden, joy's never done.

The Luminous Awakening

In the morning, I stretch and glow,
Like a sunflower, ready to show.
With coffee in hand, my roots take a sip,
Dancing with joy, oh what a trip!

Laughing at shadows that once loomed large,
Bouquet of giggles, I'm in charge.
The sun tickles my skin, oh what a tease,
Feeling so light, I'm swaying with ease!

Seeds of Serenity in Daylight

I dropped a seed, what a sight,
Grew a mustache in morning light.
Beneath the sun, I hum and sway,
"Hey, who knew I could sprout today?"

Birds chirp loud, they call me a fool,
While I bask in warmth, that's my rule.
With roots in laughter, I'm never alone,
In this sunny field, joy has grown!

Sunlight's Embrace

I cuddle the sun, give it a wink,
Photos and giggles, oh how I think.
My leaves are ticklish, they burst into song,
Twirling in circles, I couldn't go wrong!

The radiance wraps me like a warm hug,
Throwing sprout parties, often snug.
With each ray, I wobble a bit,
In this light-hearted glow, I perfectly fit!

Whispering Leaves of Light

Leaves whispering secrets that tickle my ear,
"Join us in sunbeams, there's nothing to fear."
They giggle and chatter, creating a scene,
In this leafy lounge, we reign supreme!

I sway in their company, wild and free,
Sharing jokes with the breeze, just leaf and me.
Under the sun's watchful, playful gaze,
We laugh and we shimmer through all of our days!

Light-Powered Dreams

In the garden of my mind, a dance,
Sunbeams wiggle, give thoughts a chance.
Green little giggles sprout like beans,
Chasing shadows, catching daydream scenes.

With ticklish rays that tickle my skin,
I sprout my plans, let the fun begin.
Nature's laughter is contagious, it seems,
Filling my heart with light-powered dreams.

Photos float by like they're on a spree,
They wave hello, sipping jasmine tea.
Sunshine sprinkles on my noodle soup,
A veggie party with a luminous group.

Digging deep in my comedic soil,
Roots of humor stretch and uncoil.
Giggles bloom brighter in my leafy bed,
Where every pun lives and jokes are fed.

The Soul's Palette

My spirit's canvas, vibrant and bright,
Dabs of sunshine make colors take flight.
With splashes of joy, I dance and I sway,
Painting the world in my own silly way.

Splattered with laughter, oh what a blend,
Chasing the grumpy clouds to the end.
Brushes of breeze swirl in goofy delight,
Creating a masterpiece, oh what a sight!

Chuckles and giggles mix with the hue,
Unlocking the colors that shimmer anew.
With every tickle from the warmest ray,
A mural of mirth brightens my day.

In this art of life, I dream and I play,
Joyful strokes guide me, come what may.
With a pop of the sunshine, I sing and I cheer,
Creating my soul's palette, vibrant and clear.

Petals of Purpose

In the garden of glee, I plant silly seeds,
Petals of purpose sprout from my deeds.
With nectar of laughter dripped on each leaf,
They bloom into smiles, beyond all belief.

Bees buzzing softly in a dance so goofy,
Tickled by petals that whisper real loopy.
Fluttering by in a daze of delight,
They gather up joy, ready for flight.

Each flower a riddle, each bud has a jest,
Roses and daffodils wearing jokes on their chest.
In the sunlight's embrace, I giggle and sway,
Petals of purpose lead the way.

Bright blooms in my heart, they teach me to play,
With humor and kindness, come what may.
So join me in laughter, let spirits ignite,
In our playful garden, everything's right.

Essence in Every Ray

Sunbeams frolic on the ground,
Jolly little sparks with a playful sound.
Swaying through life in a dance of delight,
Finding essence in each golden light.

Laughter spills like warm sunshine,
Glows with a giggle, sweet and divine.
Each ray a tickle, each flash a grin,
Bringing me joy from deep within.

Dancing through moments, my spirit does race,
Under the sun, it finds its place.
Bubbles of bliss pop in the air,
Filling the day with their joyful flare.

So let's chase the sun with laughter anew,
Embracing the rays, me and you.
With essence in every beam we find,
Life's a comedy; let's unwind!

The Heart's Bloom

In the garden of chuckles, hearts do grow,
With giggles and snickers, a vibrant show.
Sunshine of laughter, it tickles the air,
Blooming with joy, without a care.

Petals of mirth, they flap and sway,
Dancing through moments, come what may.
Bumblebees buzzing, in silly ballet,
Sipping on jokes in a bright bouquet.

Roots wrapped in whimsy, so sturdy, they stand,
Feeding on fun, from the silliness band.
Such a riot of colors, a sight to behold,
In this heart of laughter, we never grow old.

With each silly bloom, we giggle and beam,
Life's just a garden where laughter's the theme.
So let's raise a toast to this wild, happy sprite,
In the heart's sweet bloom, everything feels right.

Roots of Radiance

Deep in the soil, where the giggles thrive,
Roots wriggle and tickle, oh, they come alive!
Chasing the worms, in a game of surprise,
With every new twist, a comedy prize.

They stretch and they twirl, those roots in the deep,
Laughing with fungi, a secret to keep.
Nurtured by chuckles and sunshine's bright glow,
Transporting good vibes wherever they go.

In the dark of the earth, they wiggle with glee,
Sharing their stories with little bumblebee.
Each whispering leaf joins the humor parade,
In the roots of radiance, memories are made.

So dance with your roots, let the jesters unite,
For laughter grows stronger, just feel the delight.
Beneath the bright surface, where the giggles begin,
In the roots of emotion, let the fun never thin.

Dancing with the Delicate Dawn

Oh, the dawn is a dancer, so light on her feet,
With morning's soft laughter, she glimmers and leaps.
Tickling the flowers with each gentle sway,
Inviting us all to join in her play.

The sun joins the party, in bright, bold attire,
Spinning and twirling, a festive bonfire.
With beams that will melt all the sleep from our eyes,
Each chuckle of light is a sweet surprise.

Joy splashes colors across the blue sky,
The clouds join the fun, oh, they giggle and fly.
As shadows retreat, making way for the grin,
In this dance of the dawn, let the laughter begin.

So rise with the sun, and shake off the night,
Join in the frolic, embrace the delight.
For with every new dawn, there's a joke to be told,
In the dance of the morning, let your spirit unfold.

Green Canopy of Grace

Under the green canopy, laughter takes flight,
Branches creak and giggle in the soft, dappled light.
Leaves whisper secrets of fun yet to share,
While squirrels throw jokes, bouncing here and there.

Ivy climbs higher, all tangled and true,
Tickling the limbs as it giggles anew.
Each rustle and rattle brings cheer to the ground,
In this playful jungle, pure joy can be found.

Colors cascade, in wild, joyful streams,
Dancing with shadows and whimsical dreams.
The breeze carries giggles from one tree to the next,
With trees playing games, it feels so perplexed!

In this emerald haven, where spirits reside,
We'll laugh with the branches, let our hearts be our guide.

For under this canopy, grace finds its way,
In the laughter of nature, forever we'll stay.

Green Heartbeats

In the garden of giggles, I sprout with glee,
My leaves are all giggling, oh can't you see?
Photos of sunshine, I capture with flair,
Chlorophyll chuckles, floating in the air.

With every blush of sunlight, I dance in my pot,
Tickling my roots while I plot and I plot.
Sipping on raindrops, I slurp with delight,
Turning water to joy, from morning till night.

Here comes the wind, with a tickle and tease,
Blowing my branches much like a breeze.
I sway to the rhythm, a jig in the sun,
In this leafy fiesta, we're all here for fun!

Let's rock out together, in the luminous glow,
Grooving with flowers, and seeds all in tow.
In this chlorophyllic carnival, I reign supreme,
With laughter and sunshine, I chase every dream.

The Vital Breath of Nature Within

In the café of green, we sip sweet air,
With leaves as our baristas, without a care.
They blend light and love, a quirky brew,
Chlorophyll latte, just for me and you!

Dancing with sunbeams, they wiggle and sway,
Sipping on nectar, come join the fray.
Roots doing the tango, it's quite a sight,
Nature's funky party, under starlit night.

Canvas of Radiant Transformation

When green meets bright rays, it's a painted show,
Leaves strut their colors, putting on a glow.
They canvas the world, with each vibrant hue,
A masterpiece formed, from the essence of dew!

Brushes of sunlight, stroke by stroke,
Whispers of wind play a funny joke.
In this art gallery, laughter's the key,
Nature chuckles softly, come laugh with me!

Blooming from Shadows

In the dark corners, a giggle can bloom,
A sunflower sneezes and gives off a plume.
Shadows are chuckling, they wiggle with glee,
"Watch us grow tall, just wait and see!"

Petals pop out like surprises in bags,
Blooming with finesse, like well-practiced jags.
Oh, the joy of the day, in the light's sweet embrace,
Flora humorously thrives, keep up the pace!

Symphony of Sun and Shade

Gather 'round folks, for a concert today,
With sunbeams on strings, and shadows at play.
The leaves clap along with a rustling cheer,
Nature's own band, let's give them a ear!

Notes of the breeze dance through sunny rays,
While flowers drop beats, in whimsical ways.
Every stem's a performer, each root is a guide,
Join in the laughter, let joy slip and slide!

Light's Embrace on Tender Dreams

In the morning, sun does peek,
Tickling leaves, a game of cheek,
Dancing shadows, joining the fun,
Whispering secrets, one by one.

Bouncing beams on sleepy grass,
Laughter blooms as colors pass,
A kaleidoscope of joy and cheer,
Nature grins from ear to ear.

Nourished by Celestial Rays

When sunlight sips on dew-kissed leaves,
Each droplet dances, spins, and weaves,
The flowers giggle, can't hold tight,
Sharing jokes with the stars at night.

Raindrops chuckle, not feeling blue,
As clouds wear costumes, what a view!
Celestial whispers, soft and sweet,
Nature's carnival, can't be beat.

The Soul's Lush Tapestry

Threads of gold in the garden bright,
Stitching laughter with pure delight,
A tapestry woven in vibrant hue,
With dandelion wishes, dreams come true.

Sunflowers nodding in great debate,
Discussing secrets, oh so late,
Their petals curl like eager ears,
Fueling joy, quelling all fears.

Seeking Light in Silent Corners

In shadows deep, a mischief plays,
A little gnome with sunny rays,
Tickling toes of the passing bees,
Joining in on their buzzing spree.

Beneath the ferns, where giggles grow,
Whispers float, a soft hello,
In the corner, where the light breaks free,
A secret party, just you and me.

Harvests of Hope

In a field where giggles grow,
Beneath the sun, they put on a show.
Laughter sprouts like wildflowers bright,
Harvesting joy from morning to night.

Worms dance in soil, what a sight!
They wiggle and jiggle, much to delight.
Throw in a breeze, and oh what a cheer,
Nature's comedy, we all should revere.

Energy in Every Breath

Inhale the giggles, exhale the grins,
Life's little laughs, like tickle fights wins.
With every breath, we puff out fun,
Filling the world with joy by the ton.

Breezes carry whispers, like jokes on the wing,
A chorus of chuckles, oh what they bring!
Each smile we share fuels the light,
Our spirit's power, shining so bright.

Spirit's Evergreen

In the forest of quirks, trees sway in glee,
Bounding with laughter, wild and free.
Their leaves wink with secrets, giggling along,
Turning the branches into a song.

Roots twisted together like friends at a party,
Dancing to rhythms, oh so hearty.
Sunbeams tickling the bark with delight,
An arboreal circus, what a sight!

A Garden of Reflection

In a patch of wisdom where daisies declare,
'Stop and smell the laughter, if you dare!'
Mirrors made of puddles, reflections of glee,
Show us our smiles, how silly we can be.

Garden gnomes grinning, hiding in shade,
Plotting new pranks, oh the games they've laid!
Sprouts of contemplation, well-fed on jest,
In this plot of silliness, we're truly blessed.

Seeds of Serenity

In a garden of giggles, I sprout,
With sunlight and laughter, there's no doubt.
Watering worries with a sprinkle of glee,
Blooming wild in life, just let me be.

The weeds try to tickle, but I dodge and weave,
Dancing with daisies on a sunny eve.
Roots drink up joy from the soil so deep,
Growing up silly, not losing sleep.

The Treetops of Tomorrow

I'm a tree with a hat made of bright clouds,
Swaying to tunes that make me proud.
Squirrels tell jokes while I sip morning dew,
Branching out dreams, oh if only they knew.

Leaves in my branches, they chuckle and sing,
Who knew being tall would feel like a fling?
With sun-kissed thoughts and a trunk full of cheer,
Swinging in breezes, I couldn't be near.

Flourishing Frequencies

In a garden of giggles, let's harmonize,
Each petal's a note that opens the skies.
With bees as our band and the sun as our stage,
Buzzing out melodies for every age.

Serenity sprouts from laughter's embrace,
Dancing in circles, it quickens our pace.
Photos flicker like fireflies in flight,
Growing our joy with every delight.

Vibrations of Vitality

With a bounce in my roots, I'm feeling alive,
Wiggling in rhythm, it's sweet to survive.
Chasing the clouds that float by with a grin,
Bouncing and smiling, where do I begin?

The sun throws a party for all of us trees,
Let's dance with the leaves in the warm summer breeze.
Twirling our branches, we sway and we swing,
Living and laughing, it's the joy that we bring.

Soulful Symbiosis

In the garden of my mind, plants grow tall,
With petals made of laughter, they never fall.
Sunbeams tickle roots, oh what fun,
Photos fuse with giggles, shining like the sun.

Bees don't buzz, they chuckle and sway,
Wearing tiny sunglasses, they roam and play.
Dancing with the daisies, we make quite the scene,
In this wacky little world, nothing's too serene.

Living Light Within

A glow inside me, like a jelly bean,
With rays of sunshine, I'm feeling quite keen.
My spirit's zany, like dancing stale bread,
Soaking up the rays, while I laugh in bed.

The photons party hard, with cookies and milk,
Turning my frown into a quilt of silk.
Watch me twirl in chlorophyll flair,
In this cosmic kitchen, joy fills the air.

Celestial Currents

Waves of giggles crash, oh what a sight,
As starlight glimmers, dancing with delight.
I float on cosmic breeze, a leaf on a whim,
Spinning round the sun, my playful little hymn.

Planets have punchlines, comets crack jokes,
Their laughter wraps around me like fluffy yolks.
Gravity giggles, holding me tight,
Bouncing off clouds, I'm a feathered kite.

Spectrum of Serenity

A rainbow of chuckles, colors abound,
In the land of the ticklish, joy is profound.
Each hue a giggle, each shade a cheer,
Turning cares to confetti, let's have a beer!

Frogs in tuxedos croak in delight,
While flowers waltz in the soft moonlight.
Sunshine sprinkles smiles, like sugar on cake,
In the garden of glee, it's fun that we make.

The Light That Nourishes the Heart

In the garden of my chest,
Sunshine tickles every zest.
Rainbows dance upon my face,
While my worries take a race.

Photos are what I really missed,
Like food, they nourish—so persist!
Light-hearted jokes sprout like beans,
Leaving shadows in the marines.

Hues of Harmony and Growth

Dancing vines in my mind's room,
Paint the walls with joyful bloom.
Every giggle plants a seed,
That sprouts and laughs at every deed.

Sunbeams sprinkle on my snacks,
Crazy colors raise the hacks.
Orange, purple, green, and blue,
That's the shade of my next brew.

The Inner Landscape of Light

Chasing beams like playful cats,
In my thoughts, they wear big hats.
Shadows whisper silly rhymes,
While the sun keeps passing times.

Balloons floating in my chest,
Tickling feelings, all the best.
Every chuckle makes grass grow,
In this bright, hilarious show.

Nature's Embrace on the Spirit

In the arms of leafy cheer,
Nature hugs me, never fear.
With a wink, she sprinkles fun,
Silly squirrels on the run.

Birds serenade with wacky tunes,
While I dance beneath the moons.
Laughter sprouts from every tree,
Making life as light as me.

Nature's Embrace Within

Leaves are laughing in the breeze,
They sway and twist with utter ease.
Sunbeams tickle, making them grin,
While roots are grumbling, where to begin?

Birds are chirping their silly songs,
While flowers bloom where humor belongs.
The soil jokes, 'I'm full of glee!'
As earthworms dance in jubilee!

A squirrel spins with graceful flair,
As if he's the star of a Broadway affair.
While mushrooms chuckle in their spots,
Whispering secrets in tiny knots.

With every laugh, the world does grow,
In nature's hug, we steal the show.
The sun, the trees, they all must know—
That joy is where the green things go!

Luminous Growth

Light bursts forth like morning cheer,
While seeds below feel love so near.
In gardens bright, where veggies jest,
They poke their heads, it's quite the quest!

Carrots giggle beneath the dirt,
While peas play tag, their leaves alert.
Oh, how they stretch to reach the sky,
With leafy arms, they wave goodbye!

Radishes make a grand parade,
While sunflowers plot a fun charade.
"Look at us," the greens proclaim,
In this bright world, we're all the same!

Photos taken at every turn,
With sunlight bright, the laughter burns.
In every sprout, there's a glimmering goal,
As they all bask in the love of the whole!

The Symphony of Seasons

Spring brings jokes that bloom and sway,
While Winter slips on ice ballet.
Summer shouts with laughter loud,
As leaves wear sun hats, oh so proud!

Autumn chuckles, dropping leaves,
As trees play tricks, turning their sleeves.
The seasons swap their playful tales,
In this grand dance where joy prevails!

Storm clouds roll with playful might,
While raindrops laugh in pure delight.
Each season spins a witty rhyme,
A round of applause for nature's time!

Together they create a show,
In every breeze, in every flow.
So join the fun, let laughter ring,
In harmony, the world takes wing!

Nourished by Light

Oh, sun, you're quite the chef today,
Cooking rays in a golden display.
Your warmth ignites the giggling greens,
In a feast where joy is all that gleans!

Grass tickles toes with a playful hurt,
As daisies wear their sunny skirt.
The lilacs whisper jokes so sweet,
While shadows dance beneath our feet.

With every sip of morning dew,
Plants toast to life, all bright and new.
They stretch and yawn with laughing cheer,
Feeling the love from everyone near!

So here's a toast to light's fun role,
In the banquet of life that fills the soul.
With every spark, the world ignites,
In this glowing dance of pure delights!

The Silent Growth

In the garden where giggles glide,
Plants whisper secrets with pride.
Roots wiggle, trying to boast,
About the nutrients they love the most.

Sunbeams tickle the leaves with glee,
While worms in the dirt sip their tea.
A cactus tells jokes—prickly and bright,
While daisies discuss the bugs they might bite.

Silly sprouts stretch toward the sky,
Dreaming of clouds that float by.
With every inch up, they cheer and shout,
Rooted in laughter, there's no doubt.

And in this green, magical place,
Every belly laugh quickens the pace.
In silence, they grow, yet joy is loud,
Waving their petals, oh they feel proud!

A Tapestry of Shade and Light

Sunlight winks through leafy braids,
Casting laughter on sunlit glades.
The ferns wear hats—what a sight!
While shadows twirl, oh what a fright!

Beams ripple like water, all gold,
Tickling the plants, making them bold.
Beneath the canopy, a snail slips by,
Wearing a shell that's oh-so-sly.

A squirrel chases a radiant ray,
Dancing around in a playful way.
While flowers compete for the sun's embrace,
It's a shade and light fashion show, a wild race!

In the quilt of greens, laughter ignites,
As critters declare, "Let's have some heights!"
With pollinators buzzing all around,
In this leafy lounge, pure fun is found!

When Shadows Dance

Under the moon, the shadows play,
Swinging and swaying in a cheeky way.
A leaf's silly jig brings a giggle,
As grass blades join, and all start to wiggle.

Crickets tune in with a funny song,
While the night air hums along.
A spider spins webs like it's a show,
Calling for friends with a twinkling glow.

The bushes chuckle as they sway,
Mimicking stars that seem to stray.
Each shiver and shake is quite a tease,
As branches do their nightly breeze.

In this moonlit circus, blooms all around,
They dance so nicely, not a sound.
Just whispers of leaves on a breezy night,
With shadows that smile, oh what a sight!

The Language of Leaves

Leaves gossip loudly in rustling spree,
Sharing their stories, oh so free.
One leaf shouts, "I've met the sun!"
Another replies, "Oh what fun!"

Prickly ones whisper, "Stay back, you!"
While soft ones just flutter, "Come dance too!"
They trade silly tales of storms and claps,
While saplings giggle, curled in their naps.

In this foliage fest, not a care in sight,
They plot and plan for the next daylight.
With sunlight as their sparkling glue,
No reason to fret, just fun to pursue!

So next time you wander through woods so dear,
Listen closely, lend an ear.
For the leaves are laughing, spinning their yarn,
In the language of joy, where no hearts are worn!

Radiance in Stillness

In a garden where giggles grow,
A cactus dances, don't you know?
Sunshine tickles, all around,
Laughter blooms from underground.

Worms wear shades, oh what a sight,
They party hard until it's night!
The daisies chime, a funny tune,
Under the watch of a silly moon.

Flourishing Under the Stars

Stars wink as they sip on dew,
Trees jump-jack, it's a lively crew!
Grass tickles toes, a playful tease,
While crickets croon with joyful ease.

Moths in capes take to the air,
Throwing shapes without a care!
The night is ripe for silly schemes,
As dreams sprout wildly from moonlit beams.

Pathways of Light

Light fairies dance on dew-kissed leaves,
Whispering secrets the garden breathes.
The sun wears shades, what a delight,
As plants boogie in the soft sunlight.

A daffodil tells jokes so cheesy,
While roses blush, slightly uneasy.
And every petal with a grin,
Knows how to let the fun begin!

Blossoming Awareness

A broccoli bro claimed he could sing,
While carrots debated the next big thing.
Tomatoes stacked in a fashion so neat,
Formed a pyramid that's quite the feat!

On the vine, the grapes started to sway,
Having a ball, or so they say.
With each burst of laughter, the garden knows,
That joy is where true wisdom grows.

Soul's Garden in the Sun

In my yard, a flower sneezed,
It honked like a goose, oh please!
Plants do yoga, stretching wide,
In the sunlight, they take pride.

A sunflower did a little jig,
Shaking that big ol' head so big!
While daisies danced like they were bold,
In this garden, stories unfold.

Bumblebees buzz in a choir,
Singing tales that inspire.
The tomatoes giggle, red with glee,
As the corn sprouts "Look at me!"

Nature's humor blooms so bright,
In this paradise of light.
Come join the fun, let's all play,
In this garden, come what may!

When Leaves Speak to the Sky

Leaves gossip with the clouds,
Sharing secrets, soft and loud.
"Hey, Mr. Sun, what's the scoop?"
And the bluebirds join the troupe.

A tumbleweed rolled in with flair,
"Did you see that squirrel over there?"
They giggle at shadows playing tag,
While the breezes cheerfully brag.

One leaf claimed it's got the moves,
Gliding down in leafy grooves.
The pines stand tall, they just can't wait,
To dance 'neath stars, isn't that great?

When storms come, they cry "Hooray!"
Dancing wild in their own way.
Swirling laughter fills the air,
Nature's jokes are everywhere!

Illuminated Roots of Being

Roots underground have quite the chat,
"Did you hear about that big fat rat?"
They wiggle and squiggle, trying to find,
The lost treasures left behind.

"My friend, the carrot, is way too shy,"
Said a beet with a soft, green sigh.
"Let's throw a party down below,
Where the dark and muddy secrets flow!"

At dusk, they flicker, tiny lights,
Sharing dreams of daring flights.
With wormy friends, they laugh and cheer,
As the moon whispers, "I'm right here!"

These roots don't take life too serious,
Their jokes are simply delirious.
Digging deep, they find their tune,
Swaying gently 'neath the moon!

Essence Caught in Sunbeams

Sunbeams sneak through window cracks,
Tickling sleepy faces, what fun hacks!
The coffee mug hums a happy song,
While spoon and sugar dance along.

In a jar, light giggles bright,
As shadows stretch in morning light.
Lemons roll with a zestful laugh,
Making cheer for a sunny path.

Spilling sunshine on the floor,
The cat jumps up, "I want more!"
Even the fridge joins in the game,
Singing tunes of butter, so lame.

Caught in rays, we twirl and spin,
Life's a dance, let's begin!
Joy is ripe, like fruits in bloom,
As light fills every cozy room!

The Nexus of Life

In the garden of thoughts, I stand so spry,
There's a tickle of sunshine, oh my, oh my!
With roots in my laughter and leaves that can sway,
I'm the punchline of nature, come join the fray!

With a sip of the breeze, I wiggle and quake,
Is photosynthesizing just a big joke to make?
My branches all jive, in a quirky ballet,
While bees in tuxedos all buzz for the play!

The sun's a bright buddy, and rain's got my back,
Together we're crafting a cosmic snack.
Why worry and fret? Just dance in the soil,
Let's grow with a grin, it's our gig and our toil!

With chlorophyll dreams, I giggle and grow,
In this wacky wild world, it's a comedic show.
Oh, to be a plant, in the sun's warm embrace,
Life's a green comedy, a hilarious place!

Illuminating the Path

The sunlight's a lamp, and I'm the great troll,
Peeking from shadows, that's how I roll.
Photos pinching rays, like a lunch line on speed,
Caffeine for my roots, oh what fun do I need!

With every bright glimmer that dances around,
I'll sprout silly thoughts like a well-planted clown.
Flashing my colors, I prance in delight,
Illuminating mirth, through the day and the night!

The wind whispers jokes, tickling leaves with a sway,
Yeah, my garden's a circus, come laugh and play!
We'll juggle the sunshine, while sipping on dew,
In this patch of existence, I'll brighten for you!

Let's shine up our smiles, and frolic through greens,
The humor in nature is bursting at seams.
We'll plant every punchline in soil soft and warm,
And watch our giggles grow in whimsical form!

Soulful Sprouts

In the plot of my heart, blossoms sprout with glee,
    Twirling with sunshine, just look at me!
    Dancing in chlorophyll, I laugh out loud,
    Nature's little clown, oh I'm so proud!

With roots in the soil and dreams in the sky,
Counting the stars as they wink by and bye.
My petals hold secrets, my leaves tell a tale,
Of the frolicsome sprites that never say stale!

We'll sip on the nectar that fills up our days,
With chats from the bees and the sun's funny rays.
In this garden of whimsy, we stretch and we laugh,
    Growing goofy and grand, like a comical staff!

Soulful little buds, let's crown ourselves bright,
    In a bouquet of laughter, we're pure delight.
    Sprouting in joy, we'll lighten the load,
In this quirky green realm, we're the laughter road!

Celestial Fertility

Let's talk about planets, and dirt, and some fun,
In the universe's garden, we've only begun.
Stars sprinkle giggles as they twinkle and play,
Fertility's a joke that's here to stay!

Comets dash by with their cosmic routines,
While I'm over here cracking the silliest scenes.
The moons are just peas, all laughing in rows,
In this grand show of growth, anything goes!

With crops that wear hats and shout out their dreams,
And veggies spinning tales of their wildest schemes.
Celestial farming makes hilarity sprout,
It's a cosmic buffet, of humor no doubt!

So dig in, my friend, to this stellar delight,
Where laughter's the harvest, all day and all night.
In fields of absurdity, we'll dance and we'll twirl,
The universe's jesters, sprouting joy in a whirl!

The Quiet Growth

In my garden, seeds do wiggle,
Sunshine dances, just for giggle.
Roots are stretching, oh so wide,
Like an octopus trying to hide.

Clouds look down, they start to tease,
'Hey little sprout, wanna take a breeze?'
Grasshoppers hop, they play a tune,
While daisies sway to the afternoon.

Melodies of the Mind

Thoughts like daisies popping up,
In a mind that's like a cup.
Pouring sunshine, mixing clay,
Crafting dreams that dance and sway.

Hummingbirds zip by to sip,
Ideas bloom in a joyful trip.
Chasing shadows, laughing loud,
In the brainy, sunny crowd.

The Garden of Becoming

Digging in dirt, feeling quite spry,
Worms are wriggling, oh my my!
Puns are blooming, petals bright,
Who knew growth could be a delight?

With watering can, I sing a line,
"Grow, you silly thing, just fine!"
Roses roll their eyes in jest,
While sunflowers strut, thinking they're best.

Whispers of the Wind

Wind whispers secrets in my ear,
"Hey, sweet plant, no need to fear!"
It tickles leaves, makes them giggle,
Turns serious thoughts into a wiggle.

Every gust an airy joke,
Makes the branches bend and poke.
With each breeze, the laughter swells,
In a world where joy just dwells.

The Dance of Chlorophyll

In the garden, plants get jiggy,
They sway and shake, oh so picky.
Green confetti flying about,
Photos making fun, without a doubt!

A leaf in tutu, what a sight,
Spinning under morning light.
With sunshine, they just can't resist,
Promenade under nature's twist!

Laughter sprouts in every sprout,
Roots wiggling, dancing about.
Nature's party under the sky,
Who knew plants could really fly?

The soil taps its feet in glee,
While worms do the cha-cha, whee!
Even the wind joins in the fun,
Chlorophyll balls, oh what a run!

Resilient Roots

Roots digging deep, a comedy show,
Tripping on rocks and going slow.
They wiggle and giggle in their quest,
Seeking the moisture — that's the best!

With a wink to the bugs down below,
They trade silly stories, stealing the show.
Plant jokes exchanged in earthy tones,
While stretching their fingers, working like bones!

Every twist and turn, a clumsy delight,
Poking the neighbors, oh what a fright!
Yet they hold on tight, never lose hope,
In the soil's embrace, they learn to cope.

"Just a worm's ear," one root did say,
As they danced on the edge of the clay.
A root-bound rave, quite the affair,
With underground grooves, beyond compare!

Breathing in the Dawn

As sunlight peeks through morning dew,
Plants take a breath, 'Ah, how do you do?'
With a yawn and a stretch, they welcome the day,
Prancing like kids in a sunbeam ballet!

The flowers open wide, wearing smiles so bright,
Twirling in colors, what a lovely sight!
While insects buzz by, seeking a treat,
It's a bustling café, a floral meet and greet.

Leaves cheer the sun with a giggle and swish,
"Come join the party, fulfill your wish!"
Breathing in joy, exhaling the gloom,
Nature's disco ball lighting up every room!

So raise a toast with your green leafy friends,
To the laughter and love that the sunshine sends.
A morning reunion, all light-hearted,
With nature's humor, we're never outsmarted!

Essence of the Earth

In the garden, a secret stew,
Earth mixes giggles with drops of dew.
Moss in a mustache, wearing a grin,
Nature's essence is where fun begins!

The rocks gossip loud, they share all the dirt,
"Did you hear 'bout the sprout? It's now wearing a skirt!"

While pebbles roll in laughter below,
Each plant plays its part in this terrific show.

With every breeze, there's a chuckle, a tease,
Nature's laughter moves with so much ease.
Crickets chuckle, a comedic refrain,
As roots shake and shimmy in their earthy domain!

The sun's a comedian, bursting with rays,
Crafting punchlines in delightful displays.
Together they revel, in this verdant mirth,
Spreading joy through the essence of Earth!

The Heart Beams

In the garden of laughter, I grow,
Tickles of sunlight dance in a row.
Roots of giggles stretch wide and free,
Blossoms of joy, come laugh with me.

Leaves of whimsy in the afternoon,
Wiggly shadows, a funny cartoon.
Photoshop dreams and vibrant hues,
Petals of puns, I'll plant in your shoes.

So grab a shovel and dig with glee,
Join this party, you're invited, you see.
With every chuckle, I take a drink,
Hydrated by smiles, what do you think?

The heart beams brightly, a playful light,
Sprouting silliness, what pure delight!
In this quirky patch, we all belong,
Together we'll sing our silly song.

A Symphony of Senses

In a world of flavor, oh what a treat,
Tasting the sunshine, how sweet!
Sipping the raindrops, a splash of fun,
Every note hummed is a warm pun.

The breeze whispers secrets, oh so sly,
Waves of laughter lifting me high.
The rhythm of life plays a jazzy tune,
As I twirl with flowers beneath the moon.

Scent of the daisies, a fragrant tease,
They tickle my nose, oh what a tease!
The melody of laughter swells and grows,
Every giggle a seed that brightly glows.

A snapshot of joy, frames in delight,
Snap! Flash! A memory, oh what a sight!
Let this symphony play through the day,
With notes of silliness leading the way.

Threads of Vitality

Woven with laughter, the fabric we share,
Each thread a story, a smile laid bare.
Stitching the moments with golden glee,
Embroidered with puns, come yarn with me.

The tapestry sparkles with colors so bright,
Dancing and twirling, such sheer delight.
Warped in the warmth, we spin our own tales,
Sailing through silliness, we lift up our sails.

Knots of adventure in every embrace,
Each moment a canvas, a colorful space.
With needles of joy and thread from the sky,
We sew all the giggles, let's give it a try!

Onward we thread through the fabric of play,
Creating a quilt that keeps blues at bay.
In this cozy corner, let laughter unfold,
Together we'll knit stories of bold.

Merging with the Sun

Sunbeams tickle as I stretch and yawn,
With the warmth of the dawn, I'm reborn.
Chasing the shadows, oh what a race,
I'm merging with brightness, keeping pace.

A dance with the rays, a sunlight spree,
Bouncing and bobbing, just like a bee.
The clouds giggle softly, sharing a joke,
Spilling their whispers as sunshine awoke.

The horizon blushes, a golden delight,
Tickling my spirit, lifting me bright.
I twirl through the warmth, no time to waste,
In this sunny embrace, let's have a taste.

Merging with cheer, what a playful run,
Sprinkling happiness, oh isn't it fun?
In the garden of giggles, we surely belong,
Dancing with joy, let's sing our song!

Harvesting the Sunlight Within

With a grin, I soak up rays,
Photos turn my frown to haze.
Sunbeams dance upon my face,
I giggle in this sunny space.

My thoughts grow green, they twist and twine,
I water joy with silly wine.
The garden's full of pure delight,
I laugh at weeds that start a fight.

Fruits of whimsy sprout with glee,
As nature plays its trick on me.
I harvest sunshine, sprinkle cheer,
And dance among the buzzing deer.

My soul's a plant, it stretches wide,
With each joke, I sprout with pride.
So here's to silliness and sun,
Where laughter blooms, and life is fun!

A Journey through Verdant Ruins

In ruins green where trees do giggle,
The branches sway, they dance and wiggle.
On paths of moss, I skip and play,
Laughing at the leaves that sway.

The squirrels chatter, birds all sing,
As heartbeats thrum with every wing.
I trip on roots, but that's okay,
For laughter grows in this bouquet.

A fern cracks jokes, it's rather sly,
While flowers wink, oh my, oh my!
In every nook, a chuckle hides,
In verdant ruins, joy abides.

With every step through leafy halls,
I hear the tree's hilarious calls.
This journey brings me pure delight,
In nature's arms, the world feels right!

Illuminated Soulscapes

In mind's bright garden, blooms take flight,
I paint my thoughts with pure delight.
A canvas green, with colors free,
Where laughter echoes merrily.

With silly sunbeams in my hair,
I skip around without a care.
Each thought's a petal, bright and bold,
In glimmering fields of stories told.

A spark of joy, a swirl of fun,
I twirl beneath the glowing sun.
In every shadow, jokes can hide,
I chuckle loud, and nothing's denied.

The colors blend, they laugh and tease,
With every breath, I feel the breeze.
These soulscapes shine, they glimmer bright,
In joyful shades, I find my light!

Blossoming with Celestial Energy

From starry thoughts, I start to bloom,
Galactic giggles fill my room.
With stardust sprinkled in my tea,
I blossom forth, it's clear to see.

Cosmic rays, they tickle my toes,
As funny thoughts like comet flows.
A garden wild, where laughter grows,
And humor's scent, forever flows.

I dance with planets, swirl with stars,
Creating joy, no need for jars.
My roots are strong, my branches wide,
I'm fueled by laughter, can't you see my pride?

With every giggle, I reach the sky,
Under nebulae where dreams can fly.
I blossom forth with energy,
In the garden of my cosmic spree!

Transfusion of Serenity

In a world where worries bloom,
I sip sunshine from a golden spoon.
Leafy giggles tickle my toes,
As I dance with daisies, heaven knows!

I meditate with ants on a quest,
Debating if naps are truly best.
The trees whisper secrets, oh so sly,
Under a blueberry pie-blue sky.

My soul's a garden, wild and bright,
Filled with pickles that blossom at night.
Sunbeams sprout jokes that float like kites,
As I laugh with fairies, to new heights!

So come join my revels, feel the cheer,
With a twist of fate and a splash of beer.
In this leafy sanctuary, we thrive,
Where joy is the nectar, keeping us alive.

Radiant Rhythms

I've got a rhythm, a funky beat,
With sunlight dancing on my feet.
Photos twirling in a green ballet,
As I join in, come what may!

My soul's a canvas, splashed with gold,
The laughter within, never gets old.
A disco ball of joy on high,
Reflects the giggles bursting nearby.

Every leaf's a jester with a grin,
Tickling the breeze, inviting in.
With chlorophyll flares and heartbeats bold,
We're a party of pollen, uncontrolled!

So let's twirl under the leafy crown,
With every chuckle, we won't frown.
In radiant rhythms, life's a spree,
Join my leafy laugh fest, come dance with me!

An Inner Sanctuary

Deep in my heart, there's a sunlit nook,
Where laughter's the finest, open book.
With roots so comfy, they cradle my soul,
I'm the daisy-fied king, rollin' on a stroll.

This sanctuary's filled with giggles and glee,
Photospheric puddles, come jump in with me.
A merry-go-round of thoughts and dreams,
Where even the daisies hum fun little themes!

Breezes tickle like feathers of cheer,
As I drink from my cup of nostalgia here.
Each sip's a wink from the sunlit above,
Whispering secrets of joy, and of love.

So find your safe haven, let humor unfold,
In this funny fortress, there's treasure untold.
With sunbeams a-dancing and hearts all aglow,
Let's relish the moments, feel the joy flow!

Awakening from Within

As dawn awakens with a cheeky grin,
I shake off the slumber, let the fun begin!
With sunbeams winking, I stretch and yawn,
Kicking off blankets, good vibes are drawn.

The leaves are giggling, shaking in glee,
Their whispers tickle, 'Hey, come laugh with me!'
My quirks bloom like flowers in the light,
As I waddle through life, a delightfully funny sight.

Roots wiggle and dance, it's quite the show,
While clouds crack jokes, oh how they flow!
With every chuckle, I'm breathing in light,
Awakening magic, feels oh-so-right.

So let's celebrate this silly parade,
In the garden of quirks, where laughter's made.
When you wake from within, you'll clearly find,
Fun's the best food for a playful mind!

The Spirit's Garden

In the garden of glee, where smiles bloom bright,
   Laughter sprouts like daisies, taking flight.
   Leaves of joy flutter, like socks on the floor,
  Each giggle a petal, who could ask for more?

Bees buzzing sweetly, they dance with delight,
    Chasing sunbeams, they're quite the sight.
    With roots full of puns, the soil's a riot,
  Every weed's a joke, join in, don't be quiet!

Sunshine's the water, it sparkles and sings,
  Tickling our spirits like a chorus of springs.
    The butterflies chuckle, high in the sky,
  While worms make you giggle, oh me, oh my!

  In this spirited plot, let your silliness flow,
Dig deep for the chuckles, watch your heart grow.
We'll plant seeds of laughter, under skies so blue,
  In the Spirit's Garden, there's space just for you!

Sun-Kissed Whispers

Under a dome of sunlight, giggles collide,
Whispering secrets where silly hearts abide.
The breeze tells a joke that sweeps all around,
While shadows play tag on the warm, grassy ground.

Frolicsome fairies with sunshine for hair,
Twirl on the daisies, they're light as air.
A sunbeam appears, wearing shades and a grin,
Declaring, "Let's party, come join in the spin!"

Chickens wear flip-flops, and cows dance ballet,
As laughter takes root, in a comical way.
With each sun-kissed giggle, the world feels anew,
In whispers that tickle, and warm skies so blue.

So gather, dear friends, in this cheerful land,
Where each silly moment is perfectly planned.
In the warmth of the day, let joy take its flight,
And dance like a dervish in the shimmering light!

Harmony of the Heart

In a symphony sweet, where laughter takes stage,
Each note is a chuckle, from the young to the sage.
A trumpet of joy sounds, with a slide and a sway,
While the flute flirts with puns, in a frolicking way.

The beat of the drum is a thump, thump, thump,
As we jiggle and bounce like a bouncy little lump.
In this concert of giggles, the rhythm won't cease,
We're in sync with the beat, finding plenty of peace.

So join in the chorus, don't hold back your cheer,
The world's a grand stage, and we're all welcome here.
With harmony swirling, each heart finds its place,
As we all sing together, in a funny embrace.

In this festival vibrant, let whimsy ignite,
For the harmony of laughter feels oh-so-right.
With every heart's giggle, the world's a delight,
Let humor be the anthem, both day and night!

Twinkling Light Within

A glimmer of joy shines bright in the night,
With stars that are chuckling, oh what a sight!
The moon wears a grin, reflected in glee,
While shadows perform tricks, just for you and me.

In the dance of the fireflies, laughter ignites,
As wishes on wings take their whimsical flights.
Each flicker a giggle, in the cool evening air,
Spreading smiles like wildflowers everywhere.

And when the dawn breaks with a tickle of gold,
Our hearts leap with joy, with tales yet untold.
So let's celebrate magic, both silly and bright,
For the twinkling light within, glows with pure delight.

With every chuckle and snicker that flows,
In the garden of spirits, where joy always grows.
This light in our hearts is a playful parade,
In the dance of the cosmos, let's never fade!

Interwoven Threads of Light

In the garden of giggles, I grow,
Tickling roots with sunshine glow.
Photos tape my leaves with cheer,
Sprouting laughs from soil sincere.

Dancing daisies have a chat,
Worms in bow ties, how about that?
Each breeze whispers sweet refrain,
Happy saplings sing again.

Silly clouds above me play,
Hiding sunlight in a fray.
I cheekily stretch, reach up high,
Complaining leaves, oh me, oh my!

But when the rain starts to fall,
Belly-flops make the plants enthrall.
Each puddle makes a splashy sight,
Crickets laugh 'til the stars are bright.

The Green Pulse of Existence

In the realm where chlorophyll reigns,
I wiggle my stems, ignoring strains.
Green beings grooving, what a sight,
Chasing sunbeams in pure delight.

Funky fungi on the ground,
Disco moves, they spin around.
Lively sprouts join the dance,
With each twirl, they take a chance.

Roots are boogieing underneath,
Speaking secrets, sharing breathe.
I caterwaul to fluffy clouds,
Inviting them to gather crowds.

Yet when winter's chill draws near,
I start to worry, oh dear, oh dear!
But I keep smiling, holding tight,
For spring will bring the days so bright.

Whispered Secrets of the Sun

Oh sunbeam, come tickle my leaves,
Tell me tales of the roots and thieves.
I blush in green under your gaze,
Waltzing in luminous, leafy haze.

The bees all buzz with gossip pure,
The flowers gossip, that's for sure.
A bumblebee with tales to spin,
About the pollen party within!

Swaying branches share a wink,
Laughter echoing with each clink.
Sunshine giggles, a playful tease,
While I do my sway with ease.

In this sunlit lush ballet,
Every whisper brightens my day.
A chorus of colors and cheer abound,
While nature dances, joy is found.

Radiance in the Depths

In shadows deep, where giggles dwell,
Roots joke with rocks, casting spells.
Mossy cushions laugh and play,
While splashes of light lead the way.

Sneaky squirrels with treasure hoard,
Comedic antics, never bored.
They jiggle jugs of acorn gold,
Sharing punchlines, brave and bold.

A sunbeam peeks, with a cheeky wink,
Sending shadows into a blink.
I stretch my branches, all aglow,
Embracing the joy of nature's show.

When twilight falls, a balmy breeze,
Sends this leafy choir with ease.
As crickets chirp their twilight song,
Together we sing, where we belong.

Ethereal Blossoms

In a garden of giggles, I sprout,
With sunlight and laughter, there's never a doubt.
I dance with the daisies, I sing with the bees,
In this wild little world, I sway with the breeze.

The tulips wear hats, oh what a sight!
While roses hold coffee, ready for flight.
Birds crack a joke, the squirrels join the play,
Nature's own stand-up, in the green cabaret.

With roots that are tickled by sunshine so sweet,
I bubble and giggle, my joy can't be beat.
Petals all blush as they catch my good vibes,
For in this grand jest, my spirit imbibes.

So come take a stroll in this whimsical space,
Where every sunbeam is a smile on its face.
Let's laugh in the light, let our worries take flight,
In this garden of giggles, everything's right.

Awakening the Inner Landscape

A spark in the brain, like a bulb in the night,
Awakens the doodles, brings dreams into sight.
With sunshine on toast and a giggle on stew,
I mix up my visions like a painter would do.

The clouds play peek-a-boo, and the trees clap along,
As I search for the giggles in my inner song.
Caterpillars chuckle, tickling leaves all around,
While butterflies flutter, lost in the sound.

I bounce on the daisies, my spirit takes flight,
Beneath a big sky that's as blue as a sprite.
With each happy movement, I dance with my muse,
Creating my canvas, refusing to snooze.

So grab your wild laughter and paint it with cheer,
Awaken your heart, oh so splendid and clear.
In this inner landscape, where silliness reigns,
You'll find all the treasures that laughter contains.

Fountains of Renewal

There's a fountain of whimsy in my backyard,
Splashes of laughter come down like a shard.
A duck with a hat joined the party today,
And together, we jive in a marvelous way.

The water is fizzy, like soda in spring,
As we leap and we wiggle, oh what joy we bring!
With giggles for currency, we trade little smiles,
While the daisies put on their best sparkly styles.

When clouds pass above, they're just up for a jest,
Making shadows and shapes as we foam with zest.
I sip on sunbeams, they taste like delight,
As I frolic along in this shimmering light.

So come take a plunge in this splashy bazaar,
Where fun flows like water and joy's never far.
With every fresh ripple, so silly and bright,
These fountains of cheer keep my spirit alight.

Solaris of the Spirit

Underneath a sunbeam that tickles my nose,
The spirit is shining, and joy overflows.
With rays of pure laughter, I bask in the glow,
Planting seeds of delight for the world down below.

My heart is a sunflower, turning to play,
Chasing down shadows that wander away.
With giggly vibrations that dance in the air,
I float through the cosmos, with sparkles to share.

The stars, oh those jesters, flicker and wink,
As I ponder the universe over a drink.
With planets that chuckle at every silly face,
Nurturing dreams in this cosmic embrace.

So spread out your petals and open your eyes,
In the sunshine of liveliness, we shall arise.
For amidst all the laughter, the giggles take root,
In the solar shine of our brilliant pursuit.

Illuminated Whispers

In the garden where laughter grows,
Sunlight tickles, and the breeze knows.
Plants gossip as they stretch so far,
Sipping sunshine from a jar!

Daisies dance with the playful bees,
While dreams float on a gentle breeze.
Green thoughts sprout where joys collide,
In this silly world, we can't hide!

Leaves wear smiles, bright and bold,
Cracking jokes we've never told.
Sunlight's punchlines fill the air,
It's comedy hour; let's share a glare!

We grow tall with laughter near,
Roots entwined, we hold each dear.
In this garden, fun takes the lead,
Petals giggle, and hearts succeed!

Vitality of the Inner Sun

A radiant glow from deep within,
Gives the soul a playful spin.
With every chuckle, the spirit wakes,
Making light of all our lakes!

A sunny smile, a glinting eye,
Makes clouds vanish, oh my, oh my!
We gather warmth like cozy wraps,
And giggle softly in little zaps.

Oh, the joy that fills our core,
As we bounce like sun on the floor.
Vibrant rays in every jest,
Nurturing our hearts, it's truly the best!

So dance around in golden rays,
Life's too short for cloudy days.
Let your inner sun explode,
In laughter's light, we'll hit the road!

The Alchemy of Life

We mix our giggles with a dash of cheer,
Stirring joy in the atmosphere.
In this workshop of fun and play,
Life's elements shine in a wacky way!

Bubbling laughter, a pinch of glee,
Each potion's secret is simply to be.
We brew connections with every jest,
Turning mishaps into the best!

Spritz of sunlight, sparkle of soul,
Muffling worries, that's our goal.
In this alchemist's grand design,
We spin our fables, oh so fine!

So gather 'round, it's party time,
Life's absurdities are truly prime.
With each moment, we create the spark,
In this wild lab, we leave a mark!

Chasing Sunbeams

We're off to chase those gleaming rays,
Skipping through the sunlit maze.
With laughter bouncing, we run and twirl,
As bright moments make our hearts whirl!

In the meadow, we prance and play,
Sunbeams giggling every day.
Tickling toes and filling skies,
Chasing shadows, oh what a surprise!

With arms wide open, we leap and swoon,
Playing tag with the golden noon.
The sun's warm laugh, it's quite a treat,
A joyful rhythm, we can't be beat!

So let's keep running, no slowing down,
In the dance of rays, we wear our crown.
Chasing sunbeams, wild and free,
In this goofy rhapsody, just you and me!

www.ingramcontent.com/pod-product-compliance
Lightning Source LLC
Chambersburg PA
CBHW051700160426
43209CB00004B/964